Twenty One Days
with a
Mountain View

I0201508

Soul Reviving Daily Inspiration

Mountain View Members:
Lee Ann Johnson,
Marleen McDowell,
& Sandy Cathcart

NEEDLE ROCK
PRESS

Visit Needle Rock Press at www.needlerockpress.com

Visit Sandy Cathcart's Website at www.sandycathcartauthor.com

Needle Rock Press and Sandy Cathcart Author can also be found on Facebook.

Twenty One Days with a Mountain View

Copyright © 2016 Sandy Cathcart

Cover photo by Sandy Cathcart. Copyright © by Sandy Cathcart

Scripture quotations (unless otherwise specified) are taken from the HOLY BIBLE: NEW INTERNATIONAL VERSION © 173, 1978, 1984 by International Bible Society. All rights reserved.

Needle Rock Press
341 Flounce Rock Rd.
Prospect, OR 97536

Needle Rock Press books may be purchased in bulk for ministry purposes. For information, please email sandy@sandycathcartauthor.com

ISBN-10: 1943500088
ISBN-13: 978-1943500086 (Needle Rock Press)

To our friends & family
of Mountain View Christian Church
and the
awesome kids of Wilderness Trails!
—Lee Ann, Marleen & Sandy

I started writing these little messages
in our church bulletins
just because there was extra space to fill!

These are simply my ramblings,
sometimes tirades,
and sometimes the lessons
I'm learning or have relearned
from God
—Lee Ann

How To Use This Book

This book is separated into three sections (week one, week two, and week three). It offers twenty-one days of inspiration and activities to change lives for the better!

You may use this book in one of several ways:

1. Start with Day One and then continue daily for twenty-one days. (Christmas Day is a good day to start!)

2. Start with Week One and continue for seven days, then take a break and start with Week Two and do the same until all three weeks are completed.

3. Start with Day One and take as much time as you need before proceeding to Day Two. Some of the days have more reading than others. You may want to take some time to do a word study or go more in depth. You may also want to take more time for the activities before moving ahead.

4. Start with Day One and continue for five days, and then take a weekend break and start with Day Six on the following Monday.

5. You may also want to get a friend, or several friends, and go through this book together.

However you decide to use this book, we pray that the eyes of your heart will be opened and that you will love the Lord more deeply than before and that His love will flow through you as an unquenchable river.

God only gave us two commands: to love Him and to love others. All the other commands will be fulfilled if we do these two!

Contents in Word

The art work in this book
is generously donated
from
the kids at Wilderness Trails,
a homeless woman
who wishes to be unnamed,
and
Sandy Cathcart

Marleen McDowell
has chosen Scripture verses
to go with each day's inspiration.
She has also acted as editor
and offered her excellent
writing skills in
providing daily prayers.

Introduction

Mountain View is a tiny church with a white steeple found on Greensprings Highway between Ashland and Klamath Falls. Here, a group of unlikely congregants gather to worship and study the Bible beneath an enormous wooden cross separating two large windows with a view of the mountains and trees beyond.

Before worship, we often serve breakfast to the kids from Wilderness Trails, a nearby camp for at-risk kids. Many of these kids have graciously offered their artwork for this book and we are proud to use it!

Lee Ann Johnson is our Pastor Joe's wife. She divides her time between caring for kids and grandkids, a menagerie of farm animals (including Max the pig who thinks he's a dog), working at a dental office in Ashland, and singing on the worship team.

Lee Ann began writing these snippets of inspiration a couple of years ago and includes them in our Sunday bulletins. We all look forward to them so much that we decided to share them with you.

Marleen McDowell and Sandy Cathcart are both seasoned writers who also attend Mountain View and have joined with Lee Ann to create a lovely gift book designed to grow your faith, hope and love through candid stories, real-world applications, color pages, and inspirational Bible readings.

We hope you are as blessed as we are with these writings as we welcome you to our Mountain View home. Here, liberals and conservatives, alike, get along and break bread together, opening the Word and sharing heartfelt needs and prayers. If you are ever in the area, we would love to have you join us! The coffeepot is on before and after every service.

WEEK
ONE

Crystal

—*Wilderness Trails Counselor*

Turn
line time
into
SHINE
time!

—Marleen McDowell

Day One

The Christ

So God created mankind in his own image,
in the image of God he created them;
male and female he created them.
—*Genesis 1:27*

IN THE HUSTLE AND BUSTLE of Christmas shopping and while waiting in line, I noted that as I came to each checker they apologized for the wait. Have we become a society so fixated on our own schedules that we expect others to meet our all important time constraints?

As I watched the shoppers, the checkers, and the children I had to laugh . . . God created male and female in His own Image. We are created in the image of God!

Maybe we should act like it.

In this time of rushing to get everything done, let's remember to smile and say thank you to each person we meet. And let's always remember the reason for the season—the Celebration of our Savior's birth—as we wish each person a Merry Christmas.

PRAYER:

Father, standing in line is a necessary part of my shopping day. Please help me turn "line time" into "shine time" and use it as an opportunity to minister to the people around me with a smile or a word of encouragement. Shine the light of Jesus through me and help me to see others the way you do. Thank you that you care for me.

READ:

Genesis 1:26-27 and chapter two.

ACTION:

These are good words for Christmas, but also for any time of the year. Can we take this attitude with us whenever we are out and about where we meet someone else? Think about the last checker, waitress, or receptionist you spoke with. Did you share kind, uplifting words with them? Or were you so busy trying to get your own needs met that you didn't even think of what troubles they might be facing in their day?

1. Take a moment now to pray. Ask God to bring someone to mind that you might be overlooking who could use a kind word.

2. Ask God to give you a kind word for the person He brought to mind and to remind you to share it the next time you see that person.

3. Is there someone else who could use a kind word from you today? Give them a visit or call, or send them a text, or mail them a greeting card.

—*Homeless Woman*

It takes courage to make a difference!

—Sandy Cathcart

Day Two

Making A Difference

And we know that in all things
God works for the good of those who love him,
who have been called according to his purpose.
—*Romans 8:28*

AS EACH YEAR COMES TO AN END, there is always a looking back toward the past as well as anticipation of the year to come. We think of the new people in our lives and remember lovingly those who have gone on before us. There is always the list of "wanted to accomplish" followed by the list of "things still not done." For many, the New Year brings new adventures and new paths to follow and for some, the New Year can be merely a reminder of getting older.

My prayer is, as this year begins, that we each desire to do the will of God in our individual lives; that we make the time to study, pray, walk in, step out in, breathe deeply in of those things that God is directing us to do; that we choose to not stand by in apathy, but that we choose instead to step out in the strength of God; that we will daily seek and listen to the Holy Spirit; and that we will take courage to make a difference, to be different, to grow.

May you find His amazing love and strength in the New Year!

PRAYER:

Father, you desire to conform me into the image of your Son. Help me to look forward with joy to the challenges the New Year will bring. Help me to take time for you before anything else, and please fill my heart with the assurance that you will give me strength to meet each and every opportunity. Give me eyes to see those who are in need, and make me ready to face or embrace whatever comes my way, knowing that in all things you will work it out for my good. Thank you that it is your strength that makes me strong.

READ:

Romans 8:28-39

ACTION:

Jesus maintained an intimate relationship with His Father while He walked this earth as a man, often rising early before dawn in order to spend time with Him. Do you have a time set aside, a time that you guard, to spend with your Heavenly Father? If so, Bravo! If not, now is a good time to begin!

Make a commitment to a certain time of day where you set aside a specified amount of time, starting with prayer and time in the Word of God. Don't allow yourself to read any other book or periodical until you have spent time in the Word.

Start with a book in the New Testament and commit to reading a portion each day. Pray before you read and ask God to reveal what you need. Read until you feel it is time to stop. Either the passage will be so rich you need to stop and think, or God will quicken your heart in such a way you know He is saying something special to you.

At that point, stop and prayerfully answer the following four questions:

1. What does God want me to know? (Observe the passage. What is He saying?)

2. What does God want me to stop? (Is there some habit or activity in your life that needs to go? Fear? Anxiety? An action?)

3. What does God want me to change? (Often this goes with question two, but sometimes it's completely separate. It often has something to do with changing your thought process or reactions.)

4. What does God want me to do? (This is in direct relation to what you have read. Is there an action that needs to happen?)

You will be surprised to find how well God will answer these questions if you spend regular time with Him and His Word. And it would be a good idea to continue asking yourself these questions throughout the daily Scripture reading found in this book.

Even
a sigh
directed
at God
is a prayer!

—Homeless Woman

Day Three

Mind Blowing God

Come, let us sing for joy to the Lord;
let us shout aloud to the Rock of our salvation.
Let us come before him with thanksgiving
and extol him with music and song.
—*Psalm 95:1-2*

I AM ALWAYS SAYING that people will never cease to amaze me. And truly, I am pretty sure mankind will always find one more way to blow my mind.

That being said, I realize that God and His grace will also continue to blow me away.

He gives direction in quiet ways that, if I am humble enough to listen, I can gain from it. He honors my prayers whether I am deserving of His grace or not. When I need to be silent and just listen, He takes the words from my lips. When I am accused, He gives me strength to keep going. And when it's time to let go, He gives me rest.

Our God is truly an awesome, amazing, mind blowing God!

PRAYER:
Father, you are all powerful, so why should I be afraid? Certainly the God who set the boundary of the sea can set a boundary around my troubles. Do I believe that, Lord? Please increase my faith and take away my unbelief. Open my eyes to see you in the mundane as well as the extraordinary. Thank you that you do not give up on me and forgive me for not trusting you more.

READ: Psalm 139

ACTION:

It is a good thing to remember the things God has done for us in the past in order to gain strength for troubled times. Here are several ways to do that:

1. Keep a daily journal, focusing on the good things God has done. It may be as simple as giving you air to breathe.

2. Take time to be still before the Lord and ask Him to remind you of the good things He has done in your life. Sometimes this means returning all the way to John 3:16 and remembering that He loves you!

3. Read Scripture that speaks of the good things He has done in the past and the good things He has planned for our future.

4. Talk with others about the good things God has done in their lives. This is a reminder that God is working even when you are not aware.

"But
the LORD
is with me
like a mighty
warrior…"
—Jeremiah 20:11

—Jeffrey

Day Four

A Time to Remember

Finally,
be strong in the Lord and in his mighty power.
Put on the full armor of God,
so that you can take your stand
against the devil's schemes.
—Ephesians 6:10

MEMORIAL DAY HAS BEEN SET ASIDE to remember our service men and women who have fought for our freedom. It is a day to pay tribute to those who have given their lives so that we may live in a free country. Their sacrifice went far beyond their pay grade or the benefits they received.

It is also a day to remember our loved ones who have gone on before us. They too fought a battle for each of us. Many of them worked and struggled to raise up children who would become men and women to continue the good fight, to be of strong morals and ethics, so that each new generation would help to sustain this country and our beliefs.

The first warrior, the first fallen soldier, was Jesus Christ. He, too, struggled and fought, and continues to fight battles for each of us, that we may not only have a life of freedom in this world, but also in the next.

11

His sacrifice was that of a soldier, greater than any of us deserve. His goal . . . our freedom, His sacrifice to raise up a strong people with morals and values that would help lead people to life eternal.

Whenever we pay tribute to our soldiers and our loved ones, we also need to remember the first soldier who died for us, went above and beyond, and paid the greatest sacrifice—Christ Jesus.

PRAYER:

Jesus, thank you for the work of the cross, for thinking of me when you made that supreme sacrifice. And thank you for those who have gone before me, the ancient ones, who maintained faith in the face of great conflict. Please help me remember the ultimate sacrifices of those who went before me, and help me put on your full Armor so I can fight the battles of temptation and compromise in my own life. Let me stand firm when the day of trouble comes. And let me finish the race well, hearing those words, "Well done, good and faithful servant." Thank you that though this is impossible for me to do in my own strength, it is totally doable for you.

READ:

Galatians 6, Hebrews 11 and Ephesians 6

ACTION:

Whether or not it is Memorial Day, now is a good time to remember the warriors who have had a part in your life.

1. Thank God for the work of the cross — for the supreme courage and strength it took for Him to finish the battle against death and sin.

2. Read Hebrews 11 and thank God for the people who have gone before us, who stood strong in the face of great adversity and paved the way for us to be free. Go back and read some of their stories in the Old Testament. Take courage from their strength and learn from their mistakes.

3. Thank God for the prayer warriors among your family and friends who prayed you into the Kingdom and/or hold you up now. If you don't know who they are, ask the Lord to show you, then be still before Him until some names come to mind.

Seek
not to
understand
that you
may believe,
but believe
that
you may
understand.

—St. Augustine

Day Five

What Do I Believe?

Let us hold unswervingly
to the hope we profess,
for he who promised is faithful.
—*Hebrews 10:23*

THE SONG, "I BELIEVE IN JESUS," has managed to stay in my head all week long, so I figured God wanted me to truly think about the words.

The song states what I believe and then what He's done for me. But then the question came to my mind, "How much do I believe?" What are my boundaries and limits? Do I have other gods?

As the song has not stopped going through my head, I am pretty sure I have more self-evaluation to do.

What about you? What do you believe? Do you have limitations on what you believe God is capable of and who He is? Do you have other gods such as money, possessions and activities? Do these things squeeze out any room for the Living God?

Why not join me this week in asking God to reveal, "What do I really believe?"

PRAYER:

Lord, please show me the truth of what I really believe. Reveal the things and activities that are taking me away from you and please show me where my faith is weak. Let me see the truth of who you really are—Loving Creator, Wonderful Counselor, Perfect Truth, Complete Goodness, Faithful Father and so much more! Open your Word to me and reveal truth and help me not to listen to the lies of the enemy that weakens my faith and sends me into unbelief. Thank you that you do not give up on me.

READ:

1 John chapter one

ACTION:

1. What is one thing you know to be absolutely true about God, no matter what the circumstances?

2. How do you know this to be true? What happened in your life that gave you real assurance? (Interesting that this assurance usually comes from going through a very difficult time.)

3. Make a list of other things you absolutely believe to be true about God. (It is good to keep this list handy for those difficult times when you struggle for faith.

4. Ask others what they know to be absolutely true about God. Then ask them how they know this to be true.

Love
the
LORD
with
all
your
heart

Day Six

Lord or Savior?

Therefore, I urge you, brothers and sisters,
in view of God's mercy,
to offer your bodies as a living sacrifice,
holy and pleasing to God—
this is your true and proper worship.
Do not conform to the pattern of this world,
but be transformed by the renewing of your mind.
Then you will be able to test and approve what God's will is—
his good, pleasing and perfect will.
—Romans 12:1

IS JESUS YOUR LORD OR YOUR SAVIOR? I had never really thought about the terms, "Lord of my life" and "Savior of my life." In my mind, as I am sure in many other believers, it is the same thing. But in reading the book, *Good or God,* John Bevere makes a point that I just can't ignore.

He posed the question, "Is God, Lord and *master* of my life? Am I **submitted** to follow Him, to allow Him to be my **supreme authority?**" Those are words that I must admit I struggled with as I read them, but then isn't that how we are supposed to be as children? We are to be submitted to our parents as our supreme authorities?

I have always believed that God is the best of the best fathers, but to be truly submitted to Him, to give Him all authority in my life, is a moment-by-moment act of surrendering.

Bevere pointed out that many churches pray that we accept Jesus as our Savior, but don't mention that as we come to Christ we also take God as our Lord and Master.

Our Salvation is the benefit of submitting our lives to God as our Lord and Master. It is a simple statement that hit me hard. God does not have a democratic plan with politically correct terminology. He is the Sovereign God. And when we ask Him into our hearts we are accepting that fact.

My prayer is that each one of us reevaluate the commitment we made to Christ Jesus and, if we discover we only asked Him in as our Savior, that we re-commit our lives to God as our Lord and Master, understanding that our salvation is the benefit of that commitment.

PRAYER:

Father, Master, help me to live each moment by moment surrendering my will to you. Please take away my pride and clothe me in the humility of a servant so that your will works through my thoughts, my words, and my deeds.

READ:

Luke 9:18-27

ACTION:

Have you taken Christ as your Lord and Master? Yes, this means making Jesus your boss. It is good to take time and evaluate where we are on this because other "gods" often sneak into our lives.

1. Take some time to be still before God and ask Him what areas of your life are still not surrendered to Him. Perhaps it's in the area of finances or control, worry or stress. Maybe you are afraid to give Him your dreams or goals. These things nearly always have something to do with a lack of faith in some aspect of God's character. Ask God to reveal Himself more to you in these areas and to give you the strength to be willing to allow change.

2. Time is our most precious commodity. Taking a few moments to make a list of where most of our time is spent will reveal what is most important in our lives. We may think something else is more important, but time spent reveals the truth. Make your list and then prayerfully go over it, asking yourself if the time spent is in direct correlation with Jesus being Lord and Master of your life. If that is true, then time serving others, including your family, will be high on the list. Big chunks of time spent on other things will reveal "gods" that have snuck into your life.

Love
is
a
choice!

Day Seven

Choosing Love

> These commandments that I give you today
> are to be on your hearts.
> Impress them on your children.
> Talk about them when you sit at home
> and when you walk along the road,
> when you lie down and when you get up.
> —*Deuteronomy 6:6-9*

SOMETIMES THOSE IN THE WORLD do better than us. For example, yesterday, as I was helping our daughter and her family pack up to move to their new home, I noticed that in the midst of all the craziness of the day, my son-in-law would stop for just a minute to tell his son or daughter he loved them or to speak of how awesome some trick was that they were doing on a toy.

As I watched this interaction go on throughout the day I knew these children would always know above all that they are loved by their father, that he always had a moment to stop what he was doing to watch them, and to take the time to wrap them in hugs and kisses. He is not a Christian man raised by Godly principles; he is very much in and of the world. I wondered what it would be like if all fathers took advantage of such moments to praise, love, and lift up their children instead of the constant,

"I'm too busy!" or "Don't do that!" or "Don't bother me!" What would all these children be like?

God gives us His ear all the time. He gives us His time all the time. And He gives us His love all the time. When He says, "No," it's because He knows what is best for us and so His "No," is always said in love, not condemnation.

PRAYER:

Father, it takes time to train up a child in the way they should go. Help me to take the time to sit, walk, lie down or get up with my children. So that morning, noon, or night, together we will learn your ways.

READ:

Hebrews 12

ACTION:

1. Take a moment to ask the Lord if you are loving others in the way He loves — giving of your ear, giving of your time, giving of your self — especially with those who live in the same home as you. Ask Him to strengthen you in weak areas. What is one area where you could improve? Can you rearrange your schedule to accommodate that change?

2. Take a moment to encourage someone today. Send them a text or greeting card, telling them how much you admire or appreciate them.

3. Are you taking advantage of God's ear? His time? His love? Who is the first person you call or run to when you are emotionally hurt? God is our Wonderful Counselor, always available, and He knows everything. Take a few moments to rest in His love.

WEEK TWO

Crystal

—*Wilderness Trails Counselor*

People are
the only
things we
take to
heaven with
us . . . so
why do we
spend so
much time
on
everything
else?

—Sandy Cathcart

Day Eight

Levels of Life and Love

You shall have
no other gods
before me.
—*Deuteronomy 5:7*

WE ARE TO LOVE, obey, and honor God above all other things in our lives . . . and for the most part we do . . . most of the time.

Next we are to love, honor and respect our spouses above all else in our lives, holding them as a blessing second only to God.

Next our children.

Then the ministry God has given us.

And lastly our jobs and everything else.

This seems like such an easy thing to do, keeping our lives in order. But how often do we place jobs, activities, finances and just plain stuff ahead of God, our spouse, our children, and our ministry? Then we become frustrated and confused, not understanding why things have gone awry. The world says that if we are good, work hard, and are kind to others, then we are a deserving person. Many people believe this and then become angry when life gets hard and they feel as if God doesn't care, that He hasn't listened to their prayers.

We were given a map not just to salvation but also to daily priorities, to a blessed life. When any part is out of order, then our walk and the blessings of God become elusive and hard to hold onto.

We must begin with our relationship with God. Then we can expand that to the next person closest to us. For married people that would be a husband or wife, then extending to children. Once that is working then we enlarge the circle to the next level and the next. We humans act as if it were a race in which we can cut corners or skip steps, or we think that these steps are not important or that they aren't meant for today.

Really?

Did we ask God about this?

PRAYER:

Father, you know my heart and that I desire to seek you above all else, yet I fail in this so many times. Please help me to seek you first, and let me align with your plan for my life. Give me genuine love and respect for others, even when I don't see it in return. Help me to stop and take time for my spouse and children and others close to me, especially when they are in need. Help me to delight in them as you do. Help me not to allow any outside activities, no matter how good they are, to rob my family and the people most important to me of their time. I cannot maintain this in my own strength but thank you for Holy Spirit power!

READ:

Deuteronomy 4:32-40 & 5:1-33 and Matthew 6:33

ACTION:

1. Make a list of the people closest to you and place them in priority: husband or wife first; children second; others you are responsible for third; best friend fourth, etc. Now, take your list in prayer to God asking Him to reveal what the list actually looks like. For instance, is your spouse way down on the list instead of being at the top? Next, ask God to show you how to make good changes.

2. Ask your spouse or whoever is at the top of your list to either give you a list of ten things or tell you a few things that you could do to make them feel loved. I did this with my husband years ago and was stunned by the three most important things he gave me: 1) Drop everything and greet him when he returns home from work. 2) Make his breakfast. 3) Send him off to work with a kiss and a lunch. All doable things and a whole lot less than I was already doing.

3. We each have a sphere of influence that often goes beyond our immediate family. There will be times when that outside sphere will demand more time, but it is important that the number one person on your list agrees to the time spent there. If they consistently feel left behind, it is a good sign something is out of order. Times like these will cause you to feel frustrated and overwhelmed. This is ALWAYS a time to stop and pray.

It is for freedom that Christ has set us free.

—Galatians 5:1

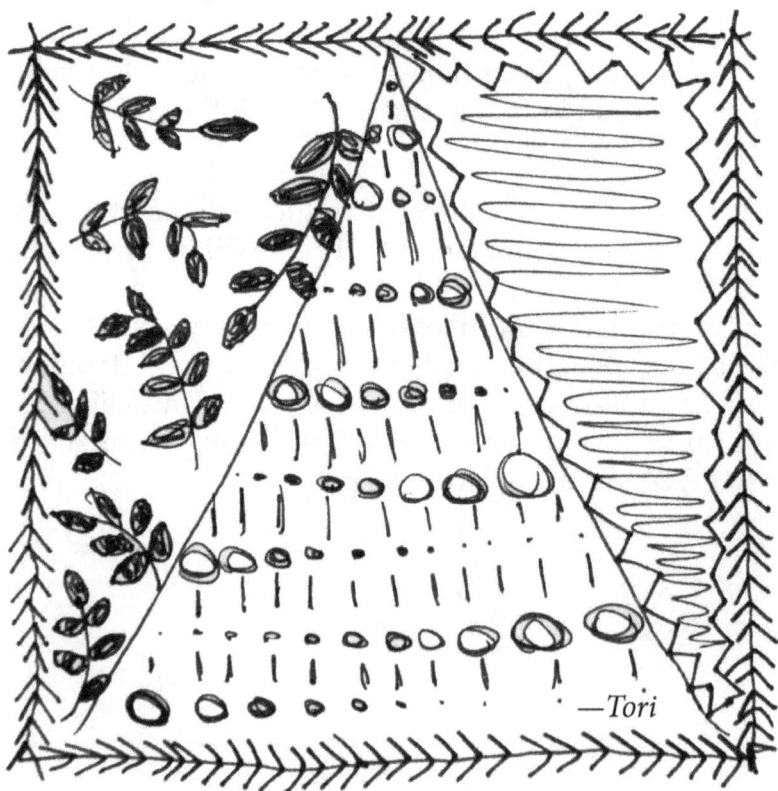

—Tori

Day Nine

Independence Day

> But seek first his kingdom
> and his righteousness
> and all these things
> will be given to you as well.
> —*Matthew 6:33*

WHENEVER I DRIVE BY THE ENORMOUS FLAG on I-5, I am filled with pride each time I see it blowing gloriously in the wind for the country in which I am blessed to live. It is a reminder of the freedoms I still have.

We are blessed by the sacrifices of the men and women who have given of themselves and their lives for the freedom that we as Americans have today. It is our privilege and responsibility as Americans to speak the truths of our forefathers and the spiritual ideals of this country regardless of what is being taught or allowed in our schools and government.

Our supreme blessing is the sacrifice of Christ Jesus who hung on the cross so we would know eternal freedom. It is our privilege and responsibility as Christians to share His Word, His love, and His truth with at least the same pride we have in our country as Americans. I think of the quote by Charles Stanley, "This year as those of us in the United States celebrate our national Independence, remember the sacrifice the Christ made to give us true hope and freedom."

We should be filled with pride in our Savior, the gifts He has given us, the blessings He has bestowed upon us, and the land He has given us. It should be at least the same pride as when we see our flag waving or when we sing our national anthem.

We are a blessed people and should never take for granted the freedom and the independence that we have been given by those who have given it all.

PRAYER:

Lord, help me to honor those you have placed in authority over me, to love my fellow believers, and to walk in reverence with you through my words and service. Let your grace flow through me so I can care and pray for the people who disagree with my faith so they can see you and know the one true God. Help me to be grateful for all you've given me and to remember to pray for my brothers and sisters throughout the world.

READ:

Galatians 5

ACTION:

Christ has given His life for us and called us to be free, but He has not freed us in order for us to indulge in our selfish passions, but rather so that we may serve one another in love. In what ways are you using your freedom to serve and love others?

1. Jesus says to love others as ourselves. Take a moment to think of something you wish someone would do for you. Then take another moment and prayerfully ask God

who would be blessed by that same task if you did it for them. Then ask God to help you carry it out or arrange for someone who can.

2. God has given each of us gifts. Perhaps you know yours? Are you good at sewing? Fixing cars? Baking? Bookkeeping? Ask God to reveal to you someone who would be truly blessed if you served that person with your gift. If at all possible do it anonymously and don't tell anyone about it. You will discover that it truly is more blessed to give than receive.

3. The next time you wish someone would phone you or come for a visit, ask God to reveal someone you know who would blessed if you phoned or visited them. Then follow through.

4. The next time you are in a group and feel alone and left out, ask God to reveal to you someone else who feels the same way. Then ask God for the strength and courage to introduce yourself. If the first person doesn't respond, try another person. Don't allow shyness or lies from the enemy to keep you from it. This was difficult for me in the beginning, because I am innately a shy, reserved person, but through overcoming my shyness I have gained a wealth of friends.

Make the

most

of every

opportunity!

Day Ten

Customer Service

Therefore, as God's chosen people,
holy and dearly loved,
clothe yourselves with compassion,
kindness, humility, gentleness and patience.
—Colossians 3:12

AS I STAND IN LINE waiting my turn to buy my items, I watch most of the cashiers doing what cashiers do, scanning one item after the next and never looking up. They are going through the drudgery of their jobs just to get a paycheck. Conversely, some cashiers are very chatty, often to the point the line barely moves and people become impatient.

Retail stores, phone, and cable companies are now asking customers to take a survey on the performance of their worker's jobs. Now, I realize that often some of the cashiers and phone reps for these businesses could use some direction as to what customer service really means, but more so, I think the companies may need to take a closer look at themselves and their own functioning in serving people.

Jesus was sent as God's Customer Service Rep. The business — Salvation.

Jesus had in all ways the most aggravating job. He dealt with people every day — the hurting, the angry, the thieves, the liars — and then let's not forget the priests and the politicians!

We are to do all things as unto God — all things! Something we all struggle with from time to time is showing a lack of customer service. Sometimes we need to step back and look at ourselves and look at our own function in servicing God.

Do our actions and words in all situations show respect, appreciation, and joy? Or are we just going through the drudgery of life to reach the end?

And what will God say when we get there? Will we get a bonus? Or will He even know who we are?

PRAYER:

Jesus, you are the creator of the universe and yet a servant to all. Lord, give me the attitude of joy as I follow your example and serve others. Help me treat them as I would like them to treat me. Remind me to share a kind act or word.

READ:

Colossians 3:1-17

ACTION:

Sometimes our daily lives become drudgery, and we find ourselves simply going through the motions and not truly living. At such times we miss seeing God in the unexpected places and joy is far from us. Here are a few things to help at such times.

1. Ask God if you are doing what He wants you to do. If you aren't sure, then ask some close friends or family members if they think you are on the right path. Pray about it and see if you have peace about what you are doing.

2. If you have assurance and/or peace about what you are doing but still find it drudgery, ask God to help you be more content and to discover the joy of serving Him at all times. Ask Him to readjust your attitude. Pray as soon as you rise in the morning, asking God to help you make the most of every opportunity. Then strive to be more aware as you continue in your current position.

3. If you don't have assurance or peace, then ask God which direction He would like to take you. Ask Him to open doors He wants opened and close doors He wants closed and to give you the ability to hear His voice saying, "This is the way, walk in it." Be patient and give yourself time to look for new opportunities, but while you are looking ask God to help you to be content where you are meanwhile, making the most of every opportunity.

4. If you know you should be doing something different but fear is keeping you from it, then make a list, writing the bad things that could happen as a consequence on one side and the good things on the other. Then pray over the list and see if the good outweighs the bad. This doesn't mean there will necessarily be more items on the good side, but it does mean the reward should be greater. What is most important to you? Does that line up with God's will? Pray it through and step out in faith, one step at a time.

"Before we look around, we need to look within."
— *Rick Booye*

—*Crystal*

Day Eleven

But For Grace

I know what it is to be in need,
and I know what it is to have plenty.
I have learned the secret of being content
in any and every situation,
whether well fed or hungry,
whether living in plenty or in want.
—Philippians 4:12

DRIVING THROUGH TOWN early one morning I watched as a homeless man crossed the street with his shopping cart to meet another very thin, filthy, homeless man. They exchanged something—cigarettes, drugs—I couldn't tell. The morning was brisk and I was sure the man had been sleeping behind some local business. As I drove past, I thought about John Bradford who was burned at the stake in 1555 and how he said, "There but for the grace of God go I."

The huge number of homeless people living in our little community often frustrates me. They are mostly young people who seem to have chosen not to participate in society. I've always seen them as self focused. But then, here were these men reaching out to one another. Watching them, I knew if it were not for God's grace, I could be in the same place—cold, hungry and confused—any of us could.

Recently, the AMC Awards honored Glenn Campbell who is now suffering from Alzheimer's. They spoke of the grace he exhibited on his farewell tour, even singing a song of not remembering. It brought to mind family members and so many of the patients in the dental office where I work who, though their bodies still remain with us, have long ago left. It is no longer possible to hold a conversation with them. In this too, "There but for the grace of God go I."

We can look at all the problems of today—social, mental, and physical—and be grateful that at least at this moment we have a home, we have family and friends who love us, and we have our mental and physical facilities. But as life goes on any and all of this can change in the blink of an eye.

Let us be grateful for what we have this moment; let us take time to let our loved ones and friends know we care; and let us thank God for all He has provided. There are many out there whose life and health are a struggle. It's not for us to judge why, it's for us to send up prayers for those in need. I truly believe that when God looks at those of us who are hurting He cries with our pain, our sorrows, and our illnesses.

We never know what tomorrow will bring. So let's be grateful for today.

PRAYER:

Father, there are so many needy people around me! Please search my heart and give me eyes to see the wealth of gifts you have given me and not focus on what I don't have. Help me not miss opportunities of helping others who are truly in need. Give me eyes to see where I can make a difference and the courage and strength to carry it out. Help me never to think of anyone as "less" than myself. Teach me to have a thankful heart and to trust you for my future as well as for the needs of today.

READ:
Philippians 4

ACTION:
1. For the next month, begin your day by thanking God for one thing in your life. Start a list and keep adding to it until you have an entire month's of gratefulness at your fingertips!

2. The next time you see a street person, instead of driving by and turning the other way, ask God if there is anything you need to offer them. Sometimes, it is as simple as a smile and acknowledgement.

3. Find a local shelter or organization that works with youth, the aged, poor, or homeless and volunteer to help out. It can be once a week or once a month, but commit to a time and keep it!

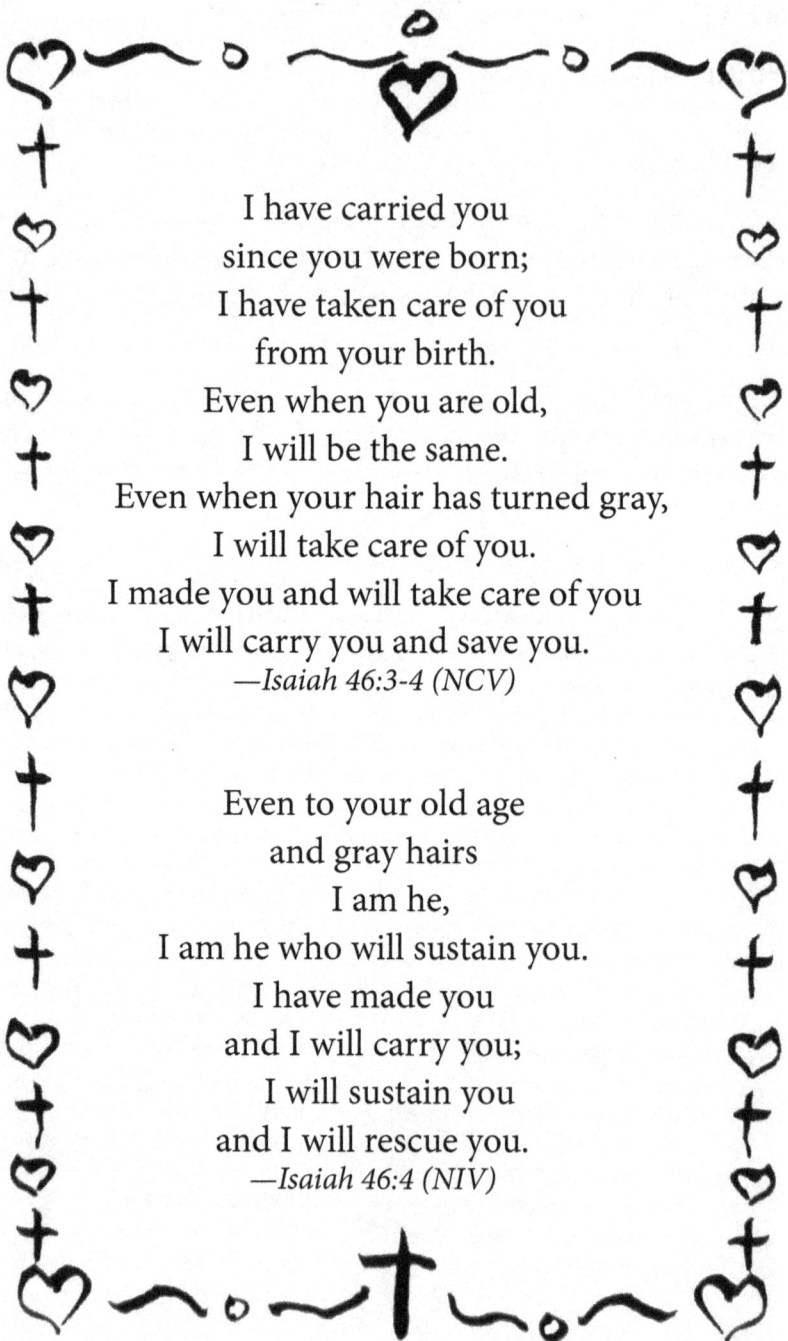

I have carried you
since you were born;
I have taken care of you
from your birth.
Even when you are old,
I will be the same.
Even when your hair has turned gray,
I will take care of you.
I made you and will take care of you
I will carry you and save you.
—*Isaiah 46:3-4 (NCV)*

Even to your old age
and gray hairs
I am he,
I am he who will sustain you.
I have made you
and I will carry you;
I will sustain you
and I will rescue you.
—*Isaiah 46:4 (NIV)*

Day Twelve

How Old Do You Feel?

So will it be with the resurrection of the dead.
The body that is sown is perishable,
it is raised imperishable;
it is sown in dishonor,
it is raised in glory;
it is sown in weakness,
it is raised in power;
it is sown a natural body,
it is raised a spiritual body.
—*I Corinthians 15:42*

IN A ROOM FILLED WITH PEOPLE from six-weeks old to nearly ninety, I watched with joy in the festivities. The little ones ran around with shouts of excitement while the older ones took it all in.

I remembered my mother, when she was in her late 70's, saying she felt the same as when she was 35, but she didn't have as much energy. I realize that in my mind's eye I don't look or feel 60 and am sometimes surprised by what I see in the mirror and what I can no longer accomplish.

In the book, *Heaven Is Real*, the little boy saw grandparents who had passed on, and they didn't appear to him as old people. They looked quite young as they had in photos of when they were in their twenties. So, I have pondered if our heavenly bodies are just the younger version of ourselves. Did God give us this little gift of youthful thinking because we were really never meant to be old?

Most of the people I see with dementia revert to places in their youth. Is this because we are being gifted through aging with the ability to appreciate that which we took for granted when we were younger? In heaven, will God meld together our youthful bodies with the wisdom that goes beyond physical age?

Most of us believe we will be literally jumping for joy, full of unbound excitement and love, when we see Jesus. I'm thinking it may be possible that this this feeling younger than we are is actually a part of God's miraculous plan.

PRAYER:

Father, thank you for your promise of a new and eternal body that keeps me young inside. Let me use all my years to serve and praise you so that I may finish my race well.

READ:

Revelation 21 and 22

ACTION:

1. Who are some of the aging people in your life? They won't be around forever. Take time to phone and tell them how much you love and appreciate them. Set aside a chunk of time to linger on the phone and make them feel special.

2. Ask an older person to tell you what it was like when they were young. Stay tuned in while they tell you their story, you will be surprised what you learn.

3. Take extra care with the older people you come in contact with today. What can you do to make them feel loved?

4. If you are aging, thank God for the hope of a new, incorruptible body that will never fail or get sick, and then ask Him to help you finish your race well. What young person can you reach out to today?

Turn around and face God!

—Rick Booye

Day Thirteen

Our Heart's Desire

Love the Lord your God
with all your heart
and with all your soul
and with all your mind
and with all your strength.
—*Mark 12:31*

WHEN MOSES BROUGHT THE ISRAELITES out of Egypt, God wanted to be with His people, to reveal Himself to them. He told them to throw off all that was of Egypt, to give up everything they had ever known, and come close to Him. As I think about that setting, that offer of God, to come near His people so they could intimately know Him, it seems as if they were truly crazy to not want that. Yet, as much as they desired God, they desired the life they once had even more.

If we were standing in that moment of meeting God, and knowing that it would change what we know of our lives, would we be ready and willing to meet Him?

God instructed Moses to take His people to the desert for the greatest Gift possible, and they pleaded that He not reveal Himself to them. Are we in the desert waiting for God? Or are we hiding from Him ready to run back to what we know, what we are comfortable with, even if it means persecution and pain?

Is the greatest desire of our hearts to know God intimately? Or do we hide for fear of what He might ask of us? Do we tremble in terror to meet the One who knows every part of who we are? Are we afraid of seeing ourselves in His eyes? He is asking us moment-by-moment of every day to meet Him in the desert, to put down everything we know, to lay aside who we think we are, and to see into His eyes—not what we are in this world—but who we are in Him.

He is there so that we might trade our soiled garments for the purest clean linens. We trade our shame for complete forgiveness. We trade our limited existence for an eternity with the Living God, our heart's desire. Let us take courage in the desert places, for it is there we can draw close to the Living God.

PRAYER:

Father, I come to you with trembling heart asking that you will burn away everything in me that is not of you. Wash me clean and set me free from the chains that hold me down and pull me away from you. Give me the courage to look full on your face and remain in your glorious presence while you do your work on me. Please remind me to view each and every morning as a new opportunity to serve you and help me to see you in all the unexpected places and ways.

READ:

Job chapters 39-40

ACTION:

1. Take a few moments to sit still before the Living God and ask Him to show you the things that pull you away from Him. Are there areas in your life where you are

ashamed to let others know that you walk with Jesus? When we sit still long enough, the Lord reveals to us where we are weak.

2. Repent of any weak areas and ask the Lord to strengthen you through the power of His Holy Spirit.

3. Now, ask the Lord what He would have you do this very day. It may be the same thing you've been doing for a long while, or it may be something entirely different.

4. Ask God to direct your steps today and to make you sensitive to His voice. Then go about your day as normal, but stop when you feel the slightest nudge to do something out of the ordinary. Does your heart quicken? Do you feel it would be a silly thing to do? Then that's probably the very thing you should do. It will probably have something to do with encouraging someone else and it will never go against His character and commandments.

Desert places become God spaces!

—Sandy Cathcart

—Arianna D.

Day Fourteen

In The Desert

The Lord is my strength
and my defense;
he has become my salvation.
He is my God,
and I will praise him,
my father's God,
and I will exalt him.
—*Exodus 15:2*

I CONTINUE TO THINK ABOUT GOD wanting to reveal Himself to the Israelites by being with them in the desert. I have always thought of the desert as being a place of hardship, the end of the line. I believe the Israelites thought they were at the end of the line when, in fact, they were at the beginning. It's when we are in the desert that we truly experience God's glory.

In my desert, I am at wits end. I have little-to-no hope, and even taking a breath is an effort. In that place where I have nowhere else to turn, when I am ready to give up and let go of everything, God shows up and fills me with His strength, hope, peace, love, and grace.

Discovering that space where He not only answers our prayers, but also reveals Himself to us, is the greatest yearning we should have as one of His children. To be near Him, to let everything of this world fall silent, and to just know Him, deeply know Him, is the most important goal of our lives.

Though I love those high places where I am overpowered by His majestic being, it is in the desert I am closest to Him. It is there I truly know He is the Living God. In the desert I have full assurance that He is always with me.

PRAY:

Father, whenever life drops out from under me, help me to turn first to you above all others. Remind me of your sacred words of comfort and give me ears to hear your voice above the maddening crowd. Let me feel your arms around me with the assurance you will never let go. And then give me the strength to comfort others with the comfort you gave me. Thank you for this comfort that never fails.

READ:

1 Peter 5

ACTION:

1. What sorrow weighs heavy on your soul? Bring it to the Lord. Tell Him exactly how you feel. Is there a person that your heart breaks for? Is there a loss you are facing yourself? Is there a worry that nags? Bring it out into the open. Is it too difficult for your Heavenly Father? Of course not! Is your love greater than His? Of course not! It often helps to view our problems in the perspective of the Living God we serve!

2. Keep a prayer journal. This is different from a daily journal in that it is not necessarily a day-by-day journal and it keeps a list of prayer requests along with dates of answered prayers. It will strengthen your faith to go back and see all the prayers God has answered. It will also help you to remember to continue in prayer for the long-haul requests.

WEEK
THREE

Crystal

—*Wilderness Trails Counselor*

god is All the time with us

—*Courtney*

Day Fifteen

Unquenchable Joy

Consider it pure joy my brothers
whenever you face trials of many kinds,
because you know
that the testing of your faith
develops perseverance...
—*James 1:2-3 (NIV)*

THE WORDS JOY, JOYFUL, AND JOYOUS are mentioned in the scriptures over 250 times, but the passage that speaks the most to me above all others is in James.

When James speaks of this type of joy, he isn't talking about facing the trials of life with laughter and glee and finding everything in life fun or funny. He is speaking about the deep-seated knowledge of our salvation, the knowledge that God is always with us and always will be. As we go through life's trials and pain—as long as we continually turn to God for our strength and remember to give Him praise—then we have persevered.

Many people accept Jesus as their Savior with the thought that from that point forward life will be a bed of roses. Not quite. The Bible states that the rain will fall on the just and the unjust alike. If a person enters salvation saying, "My name is

Jimmy, give me all your gonna give me," then when trials and troubles come that person is unable to persevere. They will end up turning away from God, because they have never truly had the life-giving foundation of salvation.

In the moments when we cry out to God, because of our suffering, we are placing our burdens at His feet. When we give thanks to Him for listening to our complaints and for continuing to stand by us, we are giving Him praise.

That, friends, is what it means to count it all joy.

PRAY:

Father, help me to remember that whatever comes into my life you have allowed and that you have allowed it for my good. Please use my troubles to conform me into the image of your Son so I can reflect the light of Jesus in this lost world. Please give me eyes to behold your beauty in the darkest of places so I can rejoice in all things. Let the praise of my lips come from a heart full of hope and real joy.

READ:

James 1

ACTION:

1. Look back over your life at some of the dark moments when you thought all was lost. Can you see the hand of God in any of them? It depends on how long you have been walking with God, but you will find yourself looking back at some of those moments and then realize that you learned some amazing truth or gained some awesome strength and courage because of it. Some of our most heart-stirring songs come from the singer's darkest

moments. Take courage from your past and hope for your future.

2. Being patient in affliction is one of the most difficult things we do in life. We just want it to end! It is in times like this that it is good to remember that, "This, too, will pass." Give yourself time. Try not to guess how God will use the death of a loved one or some horrible loss. Just rest in the fact that He loves you and He cares. Allow yourself to trust that He holds you in His mighty hands even though you feel abandoned.

3. When we feel abandoned or discouraged, it is because we have lost sight of God as who He really is. Our sight is fixed on the here and now, the finite, and often we view God as a big one of us when He is so very much more. God is Spirit and in Him we live and move and have our being! Yet, He also lives inside us through His precious Holy Spirit. Allow yourself to grab hold of this knowledge and to look forward to a glorious future in hope!

4. Is there someone you know who is going through a very dark time? Make some time to be with them. Don't preach. Don't tell them what they should do. Don't even remind them that all things work together for good. Simply be with them. Listen to them. Put your arm around them. Pray for them (silently or aloud or both).

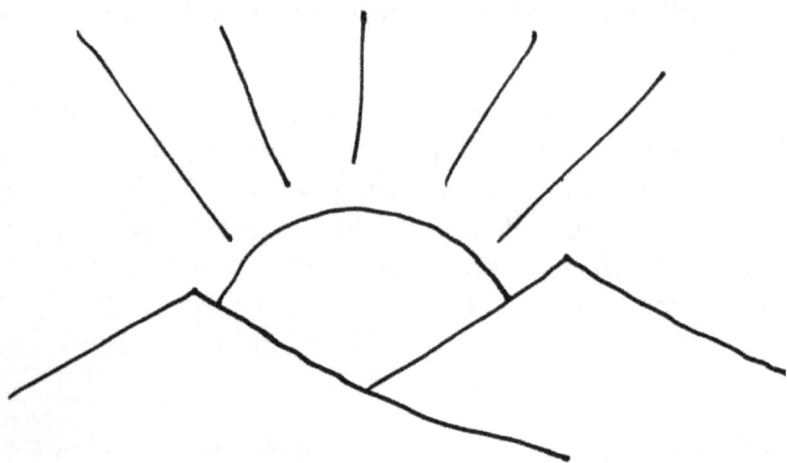

New history

New identity

New destination

New inheritance

—Rick Booye

Day Sixteen

Stubborn Will

My son, do not forget my teaching,
but keep my commands in your heart,
for they will prolong your life many years
and bring you peace and prosperity.
—*Proverbs 3:1*

MY FIVE-YEAR-OLD GRANDSON was sprawled on the arm of the couch to the arm of the chair where I was sitting with our smallest dog, Norma. As Zalin gently petted Norma's head he spoke very softly explaining to her that he knew she wanted to get the baby chicks, but that she just couldn't do that. He went on to tell her that if she went after them she would get in a lot of trouble so she just shouldn't do that.

As I laughed silently to myself, I thought of how often God has spoken to me, telling me that there are just some things that I ought not to do. The Scriptures are full of direction and yet all too often I still want to do what is not best.

How often do we later admit, at least to ourselves, that we should have taken heed?

I will forever be amazed at the human race and all we are both capable and incapable of doing. Yet I must point my own finger at myself. There are so many times I have to ask, "Was that my outside voice?" In retrospect I recognize the voice of God placing things on my heart that I failed to follow through to the end.

Our wills are so amazingly strong. The human will creates warriors, survivors, leaders, and in turn can create such damage, pain, and failure in our lives.

With all the instruction of the Bible, with the Holy Spirit trying to guide me, God's gift of free will can be a double-edged sword.

I see how much my prayer needs to constantly be, "Your will be done, not mine."

PRAYER:

Father, will I never learn to listen to that "still small voice" that gives me direction? Please give me patience to wait and ears to hear. Help me to seek your will before I act.

READ:

Proverbs chapters 1-2

ACTION:

1. Is there something in your life that God has been asking you to stop or give up? If you aren't sure, stop and ask God to reveal if there is anything that needs to go. What is it about that thing that makes you want to make excuses? Ask God to help you hunger and thirst for Him more than the thing you don't want to give up.

2. Do you find yourself doing things and saying to yourself, "God is gracious. He will forgive me?" That is a sign that you are not fully trusting God or understanding who He really is. Peter struggled with obeying God UNTIL He finally understood who Jesus really is, then He followed

wholeheartedly, WANTING to obey His Great Chief and Captain!

3. Do you have a friend or loved one who is struggling with following Christ because they don't want to give up something? Make a commitment to faithfully pray for them, that God won't give them over to their evil desires and that the Holy Spirit will continue to draw them to Himself. Ask God to remind you to pray for this person for as long as they need it.

See, I have engraved you on the palms of my hands . . .

—Isaiah 49:16

Day Seventeen

Offering Forgiveness

For if you forgive other people
when they sin against you,
your heavenly Father will also forgive you.
But if you do not forgive others their sins,
your Father will not forgive your sins.
—*Matthew 6:14*

"GOD SAYS TO TREAT OTHERS as we would want to be treated." I grew up with my mother preaching that line to each one of us kids.

So, if we are to treat others as we would be treated, then isn't that the same for forgiveness? Don't we each not only *want* to be forgiven for our transgressions and for most of our offences, but don't we actually *expect* to be forgiven.

We all walk with that deep-seated need for unconditional love, acceptance, and forgiveness. Yet do we freely, unconditionally, and completely forgive others? Do we truly give to others that which we expect of them?

Most of us have at one time or another met someone who, once they have been wronged, refuse to turn back. They offer absolutely no forgiveness, and they will hold a grudge for all eternity.

I was quite shocked this week to realize that I have been holding unforgiveness for someone in my life. Even though at one point I truly believed it was justifiable, I now realize that moment of righteous indignation has passed. All the rehashing in the world will not change it. It is a done deal, kaput, zip zap, and that's that!

But I have been continually allowing it to eat at me!

As I walked through the whole scenario yet again, The Holy Spirit simply whispered to my heart, "forgive." That's when I saw how I had gotten myself so wrapped up in my own righteousness on the subject that I have been living through a time of unforgiveness. It has not caused harm to the other person, but it has caused harm to me. I have allowed it to steal my joy and often my hope.

God tells us to forgive as He forgives. He knows the damage that unforgiveness causes, and He also knows the freedom that complete forgiveness gives.

Is it easy?

No. It is a process that takes time and God's loving hand to get us through, but in the end, if it's our heart's desire, forgiveness will happen.

PRAY:

Father, when someone hurts me, I want them to feel the pain, too. I know this is wrong. But I do not have the strength within myself to let go. Please open the fist of my mind and free me from the need for revenge. Let the healing balm of forgiveness restore my peace.

READ:

Matthew chapter 5

ACTION:

1. Is there someone in your life that you cannot forgive? Perhaps it is an ex-spouse or ex-boyfriend or ex-girlfriend. Or a friend or coworker who betrayed you. One way toward healing is to pray for them. No. You cannot pray for bad things to happen to them. You must pray for their hearts to be open to God and for blessings because of it. I've had to do this several times in my life and it works every time, even though in one situation it took ten long years before I could finally think of that person and not feel excruciating pain and bitterness. But then, the day came when I truly felt love for that person and was able to completely forgive.

2. Is there someone who has abused you? Forgiving a person does not mean that you do not take action against the abuse. Forgiving means you simply give them over to your Loving Father's hands and trust Him to do what is right and just. If the person gives their life to God, then they will become a brother or sister and you will be glad to have the unforgiveness behind you. If they don't give their life to God, then they will eventually receive the perfect punishment.

3. Do you find yourself not wanting the person who wronged you to experience anything good, especially eternal life? Such thoughts are always an indicator that we don't see our own sin and wrong doing as bad as it really is. We truly were just as rotten when Christ died for us. Don't think so? Watch your thoughts. Take note of how many times your thoughts don't align with loving others more than ourselves. I've been shocked to see how often my "first" thoughts are completely out of line. The good news is we can change those thoughts through Holy Spirit power by asking God to forgive us as soon as we think them and then replace them with something good and true and lovely.

67

—*Homeless Woman*

All misery is God unknown.

—*George MacDonald*

Day Eighteen

Fear Not

Have I not commanded you?
Be strong and courageous.
Do not be afraid,
do not be discouraged,
for the Lord your God will be with you
wherever you go.
—Joshua 1:9

I WATCH THE NEWS centered around the recent presidential election, and my heart aches for our society who are deluged with this great fear.

I see the realities of the degradation and degeneration of our society, and it has become a constant reminder of the end that is drawing so very close. Part of me is filled with anticipation and part of me with fear that I may fail God in these times. Yet I know this planet is His and His alone and if we truly are committed to Him, then our job is to do our best, to humbly repent of our sins, and to follow His lead. All the rest is irrelevant.

The serenity prayer says: "God grant me the serenity to accept the things I cannot change; courage to change the things I can; and wisdom to know the difference."

God has asked us to walk with unwavering faith, believing He is in control. The time is now, this moment, and every moment from here on.

PRAYER:

Lord, God, I pray for each of your children that each time fear tries to well up in us, that you remind us how very much you love us, that you are our great protector, our healer, our strength, and our comforter.

You are Emmanuel.

You are I AM.

Amen.

READ:

Joshua 1

ACTION:

1. Answer the following questions:

    a) What things make me angry?

    b) What am I afraid of?

    c) What offends me?

    d) What makes me depressed?

2. Now look at your answers and answer the following:

a) Does God get angry about the same things you get angry about? (Make sure you have book, chapter, verse in proof...not just one but more than one, in context.)

b) Is God afraid? Why not? What causes your fear? Do you not believe God has your best interest in mind? Is your fear reasonable?

c) Do the same things that offend you offend God? What if you weren't offended? How would you feel about the person who offended you?

d) Are the things that make you depressed the same things that break God's heart?

3. Now look at your answers and see how many of them have to do with your personal beliefs and how many of them actually have eternal value and line up with loving God and loving others. Jesus said all the commandments are lined up in these two: Love God and love others. Read 1 Corinthians 13. This is the kind of love we need to love one another with. Impossible on our own strength, totally doable with God.

4. Repent of the things that are not in line with God's will and ask Him to help you make changes to see the world in a new way, not excluding people who offend or anger you.

—*Courtney and Ari*

Never be afraid to trust an unknown future to a known God.

—*Corrie Ten Boom*

Day Nineteen

Walk the talk!

**For he will command his angels
concerning you
to guard you in all your ways;
they will lift you up in their hands,
so that you will not strike your foot
against a stone.**
—Psalm 91:11

HOW OFTEN DO WE MAKE A STATEMENT of something we believe, and then within a week or less something comes up and makes a liar out of us?

I have watched this not only in my own life, but also in others. Although there is reassurance in the fact that others have the same problem, it does not make me proud of my own lack of faith. I wonder if we all get that sinking feeling when this happens, or do we more often miss the whole incident unless someone else points it out? God asks us to trust Him and to remember that we are not of this world. I would venture that most of us think we are walking (mostly) in complete trust that God is truly taking care of our every need.

It that is so, then why, when a situation comes up in which we have stated our trust in God, do we react just the opposite? We first see the needs of this world and base our decisions on the here and now instead of stopping and thinking about what lies before us and taking a moment to talk with God, to ask His opinion, and seek His direction.

My husband and I have often sought Godly council and then stepped out on faith. Was it easy? No. Did everything go as planned or how we hoped? No. But did we make it through? Yes. Did we learn anything? Definitely. Did we see the hand of God working for us? Yes.

Even in those instances, I see that in each decision we are more in tune with the world than the Spirit. I see how God continually humbles us and uses such times to show us the limits of our beliefs. Our faith, our trust in God, His will versus our own, is often like walking a tightrope. The world says, "There is no net below, you are on your own." God says, "I will never leave you or forsake you. I will catch you when you fall. Trust in me."

PRAY:

Father, I stumble about in my faith every time I focus on the problem. It's when I stop everything and physically look up and put my eyes on heaven that the world around me is lost from my line of vision. Then I remember your promises. Then I remember your miracles of the past. Then I remember to praise you in all things because I have the assurance that you are my **"refuge and strength, an ever-present help in trouble. Therefore I will not fear, though the earth give way and the mountains fall into the heart of the sea..."**

READ:

2 Corinthians 4

ACTION:

1. Do you have someone in your life that can hold you accountable? A friend or spouse that you can ask to tell you when you aren't living up to the things you have spoken? Ask them to do this very thing for you and then when they point things out, try not to make excuses. Keep your mouth shut and take time to consider their critique. Thank them and take it to prayer.

2. Are you facing a trial right now? Perhaps at work or school? Prayerfully take stock of your situation. Are you doing the things you always tell other people to do when you see them in a similar situation? Are you trusting God? Or are you resorting to human understanding? God's solutions are most often counterintuitive, meaning they aren't the ways we would choose with our own understanding. Is God asking you to be still before Him?

What does love look like?
It has the hands to help others.
It has the feet to hasten to the poor and
needy. It has eyes to see misery and
want. It has the ears to hear the sighs
and sorrows of men.
That is what love looks like.

—St. Augustine

Day Twenty

It's Not My Problem

The Spirit of the Lord is on me,
because he has anointed me
to proclaim good news to the poor.
He has sent me to proclaim
freedom for the prisoners
and recovery of sight for the blind,
to set the oppressed free.
—*Luke 4:18*

IN EVERY STEP of everyday life we see the fall of mankind. We see the failure of the family; the failure to care; and the failure to be part of a solution. Instead, we see the attitude of, "It's not my problem," or "As long as I get what I want or need is all that matters."

We find frustration in all the wrongs we see happening, and our hearts ache over the disregard of faith and humanity . . . not only in the world . . . but also within the Christian community itself.

Yet during seasons of celebration we can see brief moments where hearts soften and joy and hope glow in the faces of otherwise hardened hearts. In that moment the Spirit has joined in our celebration, and there is hope that one more life may be touched by His amazing love and grace.

What season are you in?

Let's make this a season where we all take a moment to send prayers up for each person we come in contact with. We may not know each person's story or anything about their faith, but everyone has a need to be brought before the Father.

Today, your silent prayer may create a miracle in the life of a hurting soul.

PRAYER:

Lord, thank you for all the awesome things you do in our lives. We are so privileged to live in such a free country and be able to read your Word whenever we want. We have food to eat, air to breathe, and beauty to see. Yet, there are many among us who struggle with even the most basic needs. Please, help me to see them as you do. They are important to you and loved by you. Help me not to pass by without even seeing them. Remind me to pray for them and show me how to pray through the power of your Holy Spirit. Thank you for allowing me to be part of a miracle. What fun heaven will be when we get to see how some of these prayers changed things!

READ:

Matthew 25:31-46

ACTION:

1. When is the last time you celebrated God's love for you? Instead of waiting for Easter or Christmas or Thanksgiving for an excuse to celebrate, why not take a day in the near future to celebrate God's goodness? Make a party out of it. Invite some friends! Choose a theme. Perhaps the "faithfulness of God," and then have

everyone bring a story to share of a particular incidence where God proved faithful. Or choose the "Word of God" as a theme and have everyone bring copies of a favorite verse to share. Share cookies and tea or have a potluck. You might find yourself wanting to do this several times a year.

2. Be a secret prayer partner! The next time you go shopping take a blank notebook with you. Ask the Lord to show you who to pray for and then, when you return to your car, write down something about each person. Go back over the notebook from time to time and pray for people. If your list gets long, you may want to pray for a few people at a time. You may be surprised how you will see some of these people again and they will seem like old friends to you.

3. Everyone has a story! Keep a couple of twenty-dollar bills in your purse or wallet and ask God to show you who is in need of them. (I recently changed this to a fifty-dollar bill.) Sometimes I give it as a tip to an unsuspecting gas attendant or waitress, but most often it goes to someone I've never met. When you approach the person, tell them God placed them on your heart and you believe He wants them to have this money. Then ask them if there is any part of their story they might want to share. Most of the time, you won't have to ask. They will tell you on their own. Don't try to tell them how to live, or even try to fix all their problems. Listen carefully, and then you will know even more how to pray for them.

Christ with me,
Christ before me,
Christ behind me,
Christ in me,
Christ beneath me,
Christ above me . . .

—St. Patrick

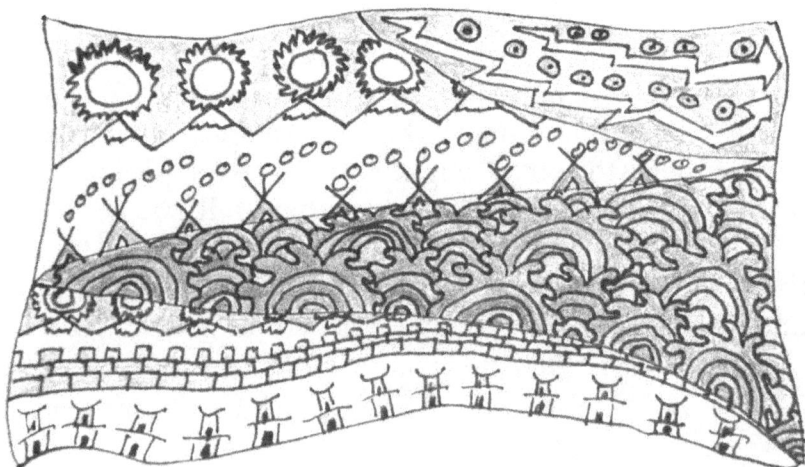

Day Twenty-One

Simeon's Moment

Lord, now You are letting Your servant
depart in peace,
According to Your word;
For my eyes have seen Your salvation
Which you have prepared
before the face of all peoples,
A light to *bring* revelation to the Gentiles,
And the glory of Your people Israel.
—*Luke 2:29-32 (NKJV)*

SIMEON WAS A DEVOUT MAN whose deepest desire was to see the Messiah before the end of his days.

God spoke to His beloved servants over two thousand years ago just as He speaks to us now. God answered the prayers of His beloved people then in the same way He does today. We each will have our moment of that face-to-face meeting with Christ but, if we have truly accepted Him as our Lord and Savior, we have already met Him. God asks us to love Him and all His creation, and to be a servant, to trust in Him and His Word.

PRAY:

Oh, Lord! Just as Simeon looked upon your face, someday I will, too. What a day that will be! To look into the eyes of perfect love and know that it will be for eternity! Please help me to run the race, stay the course and finish well!

READ:

Luke 2:21-40

ACTION:

1. When was the last time you felt really close to God? What were you doing at the time? It may have been something you did last night or this morning. For some it may mean returning all the way to John 3:16 or the place where you first met God. Return there, do the thing you were doing. Read the verse you were reading. Repent of whatever needs to be repented.

2. Are you looking forward to eternity with Christ? Or does the world have a stronger pull? Read John chapters 15-17 asking the Holy Spirit to renew your joy of heaven.

3. Is there some big thing that you are waiting for? What will happen when you receive it? Will it draw you closer to God or farther away? Simeon was waiting to see Christ. His goal brought him closer to God. Reevaluate your goals and see if they are in line with Christ.

WHAT TO DO NOW

NOW THAT YOU'VE FINISHED THIS BOOK, it is a good time to continue with the good habits you have started. We also recommend taking part in a Bible Study with friends.

Choose a book of the Bible. Something small is best to start. How about the book of 1 John? Always be sure to start and end each study with prayer.

Do some research on the author and the people to whom he was writing. What were the people going through at the time?

Read through the entire book the first time you meet. Then read through at least one chapter each time you meet thereafter. Then just take a few verses at a time and discuss. Don't just talk about what you think it means, observe what the author is saying and get some reference materials like a Strong's Concordance to look up the words in their original Greek and Hebrew. Then you can go even further by looking up some of the meanings in English. You will be surprised at how much more meaning you will receive from doing this.

Be sure to share this book with someone else when you are finished. And if you have any burning questions, we can be reached at: sandy@sandycathcartauthor.com

Meet The Authors

LEE ANN JOHNSON
As a mother of three amazing children and grandmother of four, I've learned a lot about life. My children taught me to laugh, that I could survive almost anything, humility (sometimes in tonnage), and how to love even when people are not very lovable.

My grandchildren are my payback to their parents. They bring me so much joy and laughter as they remind me that God knew what He was doing when He made parents young!

I was raised in Oregon and have lived here most of my life. Although my life goals were to marry Elvis and to be Queen of England, I married a cowboy and I'm Queen/Office Manager of a dental practice. God has such a sense of humor.

MARLEEN MCDOWELL fulfills her passion for teaching through children's Sunday School. She enjoys retirement with her husband, Aaron, at their remote home in the Oregon Cascades. Here time slows down for homemaking, gardening and exploring the mountains as she continues to "teach" through her writings.

SANDY CATHCART is a freelance writer, photographer and artist, as well as a scribe for Restoring The Heart Ministries. She lives in the High Cascades of Southern Oregon with her husband, The Cat Man, where she writes about Creator and everything wild.

Contact

We love hearing from our readers!
Simply drop us an email to Lee Ann, Marleen, or Sandy at:
sandy@sandycathcartauthor.com

Sandy can also be found on facebook at:
https://www.facebook.com/sandycathcartauthor/

Request

Reviews are like gold to authors.
If you have enjoyed reading this book
would you please consider leaving a review
at Amazon or Goodreads
and tell your friends about it!

Thanks very much!

Visit

www.needlerockpress.com
for future books!

www.sandycathcartauthor.com
for Sandy's blog and updates

www.sandycathcart.com
for Sandy's Art & Photography

www.restoringtheheart.com
for Native American Insight

www.ghostdancershadley.com
for Daily Inspiration

What People Are Saying About Needle Rock Press Books

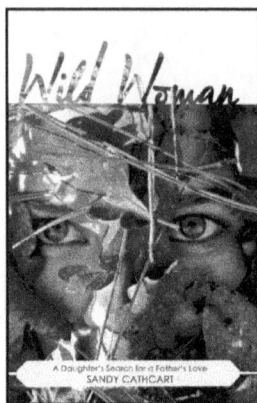

Praise for *Wild Woman: A Daughter's Search For A Father's Love*

From an Oregon Reader

"This book made me do something I don't believe I've ever done with a book before. When I finished it, I immediately went back to the beginning and started reading it again. And found new gems of wisdom the second time."

From an Amazon Reader

"How many times does the enemy of our soul whisper lies into the silence of our minds about those we love or care for? Lies that are born of misunderstandings brought on by imaginings of what we "think" our loved ones say or don't say. How many wasted hours, days or years are spent in anger over words said in a moment of exhaustion, frustration, or disappointment?

"Sandy's story is a beautiful example of what our Creator and Redeemer longs to do in each of us through forgiveness and love. When we allow him to do that in us, we suddenly become free to be loved and to give love, as he heals our broken hearts and restores to us lost relationship."

From an Amazon Reader

"This is a woman who loves the wilderness and is at home in it. She brings you the scents of campfires and forest earth, and the love of the God she calls Creator Redeemer."

Praise for *Shaman's Fire (a novel)*

From an Amazon Reader

"Wonderful book! I couldn't put it down. Written with a clear passion for Native American Culture and spirituality. In this story I found my own memories. It reminded me of so many teachings passed down to me. This book exceeded all my expectations. Keeping me riveted from page one; with complex characters and extraordinary care with details. I highly recommend it!"

From a Goodreads Review

"I did love this book! I have been a reader of varied subjects since a child but have always held a special affection for historical fiction of all genre. The Native history and culture of Southern Oregon is seldom touched by other authors. It was very nice to visit this world filled with insight that was written with the authority of the tribes portrayed.

"The mix of modern day and history keep the pace moving. A good suspense that made me want to know more as I turned the last page. The love story and family conflicts were realistic in their feelings. This was the first work of fiction I have ever read that explains the Great Creator of the North American Indigenous People as the same God that the Europeans brought with them."

From an Amazon Reader

"I loved this book for many reasons. The characters are well-developed. I enjoyed how each chapter was written from a different character's point of view. I thought it was a powerful story of the spiritual warfare of which we are very often unaware. I appreciated the way the author described native traditions, dress and speech . . . I look forward to reading more from this author."

Praise for *Eagle People Journal*

From Julie, an Amazon Reader

"Great food to nourish the spirit!!! A daily reading for each day of the year with a biblical reference should one choose to study further into the promises of our Creator. I can't wait for Volume II."

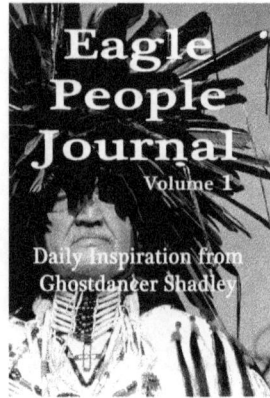

From Randy, an Amazon Reader

"This is a Christian journal/devotional that encourages, inspires and makes you think more deeply about things. And at the end of every entry, there is a scripture verse from the Bible(God's Word) to read, that seemed to have inspired the entry itself. The devotionals entry's specifically, are beautifully written and told in a Native American way. The book is also very well done, and easy to read."

From Joan, an Amazon Reader

"Ghostdancer Shadley touches your heart with daily words of inspiration on every level. Enlightenment at its best. This book is a must have for daily inspiration. A year's worth of daily reflection on a very spiritual level. The bible verse given at the end of each excerpt, gives an added lesson to be applied. Regardless of your religious background, this book is interpreted for anyone. After reading once, you will return to a special verse where the meaning becomes more powerful. A very good handbook to have for your daily inspiration."

Walking The Jesus Way

WALKING THE JESUS WAY is a term my Native American friends use for those attempting (through Spirit power) to live their lives according to the teachings of the bible (Sacred Writings) and especially according to the teachings of Jesus Yeshua.

Yeshua was not a religious man. In fact, religious people were always getting mad at him because he broke so many rules. He healed people on the Sabbath, He drank wine with his buddies, He hung out with all the wrong people, and He claimed to be the Son of God.

People who walk the Jesus Way believe in Jesus Yeshua.

To believe means to put your whole weight on this person and their teachings. That means you believe what Yeshua said enough to live according to what He says.

He says that, "God so loved the world that He gave His one and only Son that whoever believes in Him should not perish, but have everlasting life."

He also says that, "God did not send His Son into the world to condemn the world, but that the world might live through Him."

He promised that His Holy Spirit would come into our lives and remain with us if we simply believe.

He promised joy in the midst of suffering, peace during turbulent times, and hope for an amazing future. He promises to be with us at all times and forever. Nothing can separate us from His love once we place our weight on Him.

So what do you do to obtain all this?

1. You stop talking *about* Jesus Yeshua and you begin talking directly *to* Him. This is called prayer. You don't need a book to tell you how and you don't need to be in any specific position. I talk to Creator God all the time, eyes open and closed. Either way works.

2. You ask Him to forgive you for being a loser (sinner, idiot . . . whatever word you think applies best).

3. Tell Him you believe in Him and trust Him even though there's a whole lot of stuff you don't yet understand.

4. Thank Him for forgiving your sins and rising from the dead.

5. Thank Him for making you part of His family.

6. Tell someone about your decision and get with other believers on some kind of regular basis. (BTW, I would LOVE to hear from you and celebrate with you. I can be reached at sandycathcart@gmail.com)

7. Read the *Sacred Writings* (Bible). Remember to pray (talk directly to Yeshua) for guidance and direction. In doing this, you will begin to hear the Holy Spirit talking to you. The more you do this, the more you will be in tune to His voice.

When I first shared the above process with my granddaughter, she looked at me and said, "I'm not ready to make Jesus Yeshua my boss yet."

I respected Rachel's decision, because she is absolutely right . . . believing in Jesus Yeshua means you are making Him your number one Boss. She has since made that decision, and she is very glad she did! She is going for her dreams, trusting her amazing Creator every step of the way.

So are you ready to make Jesus Yeshua your boss? Are you ready to begin walking the Jesus Way?

This is a supernatural journey in a very real world. Hang onto your hat, because life is going to get exciting.

WHERE DO YOU FIT?

1. Did you just now make Jesus Yeshua your boss? If so, welcome to the family! Pray and ask the Holy Spirit to guide and teach you as you read the *Sacred Writings* (Bible). And be sure and get with others who walk The Jesus Way.

2. Have you been calling yourself a Christian but don't seem to ever get any victory in your life? Have you lost the excitement of being a child of the Most High Creator God? If so, pray and ask the Holy Spirit to renew your love for the *Sacred Writings* (Bible). Ask Him to reveal Jesus Yeshua to you in a powerful way as you read. Ask Him to help you not believe the lies of the enemy. Ask Creator God to reignite the flame in your walk with Him and give you the strength and courage to walk in a good way.

3. Did you decide that now is not the time to make Jesus Yeshua your boss? I respect that, but don't wait too long. The longer you shut out the Holy Spirit, the harder it is for you to hear His voice. Now, is a good time for you to discover who He is and what you are missing so you can make an intelligent decision. Ask God to reveal Himself to you.

"As a Lakota follower of the Jesus Way,
I endeavor to walk in the light of the Creator's presence.
I desire something akin to what the Navajo call
hozho 'the way of beauty,'
where we live in harmony with all of creation
in order to enjoy the beauty around us."
—Richard Twiss

*Return home
and
tell how much
God has done for you.*

—Luke 8:39

www.ingramcontent.com/pod-product-compliance
Lightning Source LLC
Chambersburg PA
CBHW021204020426
42331CB00003B/201